COLOR SQUARED

COLOR, DOT, DASH, OR STAMP YOUR WAY TO AWESOME PIXEL ART

LEE MEREDITH

Clarkson Potter/Publishers
New York

Published in the United States by Clarkson Potter/Publishers, an imprint of the Crown Publishing Group, a division of Penguin Random House LLC, New York. crownpublishing.com clarksonpotter.com

CLARKSON POTTER is a trademark and POTTER with colophon is a registered trademark of Penguin Random House LLC.

ISBN 978-1-5247-5895-0

Printed in China

Book design by Danielle Deschenes
Cover design by Danielle Deschenes
Cover artwork by Lee Meredith

10 9 8 7 6 5 4 3 2 1

First Edition

INTRODUCTION

If you love coloring, doodling, and puzzles, this book is for you. The pictures you'll make in Color Squared will be different from those in any other coloring book you might already have. Whereas you're usually working with flat line art, here you will use value (lightness and darkness) to create shadow and depth. Your pictures will look more three-dimensional— more photographic than most line drawings.

The image may not be apparent as you're coloring it in, or even when you're finished with it sitting right in front of you, but if you hold it away from your eyes or step across the room, it will pop out at you! This effect happens with many painting techniques, such as pointillism and impressionism, which you probably know from famous painters like Monet. The unique work of Chuck Close is a perfect example, too. These styles of art are made up of colors and values, which create shapes and depth to yield a bigger picture that becomes clear as you step away.

To create the artwork in this book, I scoured thrift stores, vintage shops, antique malls, and my own house. I wanted to find objects that reminded me of my childhood in the 1980s and '90s to create a playful, nostalgic theme. I took photographs of the objects and then broke down each image into pixels. I assigned those pixels values from lightest to darkest, which are indicated on a scale from zero (blank boxes) to 5.

There are many different ways you can complete the artwork in this book, and we will walk through each approach before you get started. No matter which method you choose, as long as each number box is a bit darker than the previous number, you will end up with a picture. I hope, as the fun assortments of objects reveal themselves to you on these pages, they bring you the same joy and happy memories they brought me!

GETTING STARTED

Before you dive in, I urge you to read through all the instructions here. The tools and techniques you use are up to you; I've tested many combinations and included the best results here for you.

I've included practice grids for you to test out some of these options (page 12), or try practicing on scrap paper before you dive into the final, large-scale grids. With practice, you'll get used to how different techniques work and feel more ready to make art. The grids don't look like much of anything before they're filled in, so if you want a sneak peek at what you're creating, check out the digitally rendered "answer key" on the back of each sheet. Or resist peeking, and keep it a mystery!

Once you've mastered some of these techniques, feel free to play around and come up with your own ideas if you want to get even more creative. But first, let's take a look at the different tools and techniques.

TOOLS

How your picture turns out will depend a lot on the tools you use. I recommend markers, pens, and stamps for this book— and I actively do not recommend colored pencils because they make the process less fun, and I want you to have fun!

■ Markers

Chisel tip- or brush tip–style markers are best for filling in the squares. Dual tip markers (brush/fine point, chisel/fine point, or brush/chisel) work great—with a set of these, you'll be able to use almost every method here.

Different brands of brush tip markers can vary quite a bit; some are big and soft, while others are narrow and firm. The big, soft tips can be pressed straight down onto the paper to make large, solid dots. (I will warn you: doing this can use up more ink

than normal coloring.) These kinds of tips are best for the methods in the book that use large dots, but they can sometimes be a little trickier or messier for filling in the boxes with color. (Prismacolor and Blick are two brands with brush tips like this.) Narrow, firm tips are great for filling in the boxes cleanly and easily, but they can't make big dots the same way, so they are not ideal for large dot methods. (Tombow is a brand with tips like this.)

Chisel tips are great for filling in the grid boxes cleanly and easily, as well as for making thinner lines by holding them with the point down, but they are not great for the large dot methods. Be sure you don't get chisel tip markers with edges significantly wider than the squares here, though it's okay if they are just a teeny bit wider—5 mm should be perfect.

Using fine point markers to color in the boxes is not recommended, because it will be tedious (similar to using colored pencils). It also won't look quite as good as the more even filling you'll get with a brush or chisel tip. But if this is what you have on hand or want to use, I recommend trying the continuous line methods on page 6 (use a different color for each step) or, if your marker has a very fine point, any of the pen drawing methods on page 5.

■ Pens

Using drawing pens (also called artist pens, drafting pens, or illustration markers) will be so much easier, more fun, and better looking than using a writing pen, such as a ball point. You can find a drawing pen for two or three dollars at your local art supply store or online; some brands I like are Pigma, Le Pen, Pilot, Copic, Faber-Castell, Alvin, and Staedtler. Sharpie pens work well, too, and are available a bit more widely— just make sure you're buying Sharpie pens, not the more common markers.

I recommend picking up a few different sizes, as different widths will be best for different methods. For a good variety, get 1 mm, .5 mm, and .2 mm.

■ Stamps

If you want to try stamping (page 7), you'll need very small stamps. It's okay if your stamps are a bit bigger than the squares (up to about 6 mm) so they overlap with each other, but make sure they don't overlap by too much! The standard erasers on the end of any pencil work great as stamps. Try a full, unused eraser for a large circle stamp, which will go outside the grid lines and overlap with the adjacent colors, or rub away the edges of the eraser evenly to make the circle smaller. You could also use an X-Acto knife to trim straight lines around the sides of the eraser, turning it into a square stamp, which will be sized perfectly for the squares here. Or carve your erasers into other fun shapes; just be sure to do so at an angle, so you're not cutting all the way down to the base where the eraser attaches to the pencil. Letter and number stamp sets also work well, if you can find a set that's small enough.

For your stamping ink, you'll need a variety of colors so that you make a set of six. The color notes (page 4) apply to ink in the same way they apply to markers.

GENERAL RULES

Color or draw in squares so that as the numbers get higher, the values get darker. Depending on your method, this will mean either the colors get darker, or the squares have more pen lines.

Blank boxes are the lightest. If you're using a pen method, these can be left blank or have a small pen dot. If you're filling in the boxes with colors in any way, these should be filled in with your lightest shade—

your art will look unfinished if they are left blank. 5 boxes are the darkest.

X boxes are the background and can be filled in with anything you want! The best way to make your image pop is to make the **x** boxes very different from the blank and number boxes. If you used a pen method for the picture, for example, you could fill in the **x** boxes with color. If you filled in the number boxes with colors, you could draw lines through the **x** boxes or use a totally different color on them—for instance, if you used shades of blues and greens for your picture, try red or pink for the **x** boxes. You can even make the background patterned with multiple colors, or draw dots or lines layered over color, like I did on the cover examples. Have fun with it!

Don't worry if your filling (color, pen, stamp, or otherwise) goes outside the grid lines and over into the next box; overlapping is totally fine. In this book, you are not meant to color inside the lines!

COLORS

If you want to fill in your image with solid colors, you'll need at least three and up to six colors that range in value from lightest (blank) to darkest (5). They can be any colors you like, as long as each is darker than the last. Using a variety of shades of the same color family is best for making a really clear image, but below are some different color ranges that can also work well.

Those are just some ideas to get you started; play around as you please! Try not to jump too dramatically from one color or shade to the next. For example, don't hop from a medium shade, such as red or turquoise, to black; instead, try red to dark brown or turquoise to navy blue for a smoother transition.

I recommend testing any color combination on scrap paper before diving into the art in order to be sure the range of colors truly is light to dark. Though the markers may appear to be distinct, the shades may look different on paper than you expect: similar shades could be too close in value, or the colors just might not look nice together. It sounds funny, but try squinting your eyes when looking at your scrap paper; squinting helps your eyes to register value more and colors less, so this will help you to confirm the shades range from light to dark.

If you don't have six colors, don't worry! You can make great-looking images with just three or four shades (ranging from light to dark) by layering dots or lines over some of the squares (see the layered color methods starting on this page).

METHODS

Whenever you see "fill in," that means color in completely with a marker. This is where it's best to use brush or chisel tip markers for a clean (and also quick and easy) fill.

When filling in solid colors or making straight lines, move your marker or pen across multiple boxes of the same number that are next to each other without picking up your hand. See examples of the methods on pages 8–11.

◼ Six-color Methods
SIX-COLOR FILLED IN: Fill in each box with color, starting with all the blank boxes, then all the 1 boxes, and so on, filling in the 5 boxes last.

SIX-COLOR LARGE DOTS: If you have large, soft brush tip markers, press straight down to make large dots so that the edges of the dots touch the grid lines, or overlap outside the lines a bit. Begin with all the blank boxes, then all the 1 boxes, and so on, dotting in the 5 boxes last.

SIX-COLOR WITH SMALL DOTS: Complete the six-color filled in method first, then add a small dot in each box over the top, each number getting a dot that is the color one step darker. In other words, dot in the blank boxes with the color used to fill in 1 boxes; dot in the 1 boxes with the color used to fill in 2 boxes, and so on. If the 5 boxes are not black, then you can add black dots to the 5 boxes; if they are black, they don't get a dot.

◼ Layered Color Methods
(THREE- AND FOUR-COLOR METHODS)
For the following methods, you'll need a set of either three or four markers, which will be used for both filling in and drawing over the top. You'll need to be able to read the numbers underneath all of the colors except for the darkest one, so avoid using very dark colors for the two or three lightest shades. In these scenarios, color A is always lightest, with each letter progressing darker.

BLANK BOXES	1 BOXES	2 BOXES	3 BOXES	4 BOXES	5 BOXES
LIGHT YELLOW	DARK YELLOW	ORANGE	LIGHT RED	DARKER RED	DARK BROWN
LIGHT YELLOW	LIGHT GREEN	TURQUOISE	DARKER BLUE	NAVY BLUE	BLACK
VERY LIGHT GREEN	LIGHT AQUA	BLUE	PURPLE-BLUE	DARK PURPLE	BLACK
VERY LIGHT PINK	LIGHT PINK	PINK	RED	PURPLE	DARK PURPLE
VERY LIGHT BLUE	LIGHT BLUE	TURQUOISE	GREEN	DARK GREEN	BLACK

FOR ALL THREE-COLOR LAYERED METHODS, BEGIN BY FILLING IN:

Blank, 1, and 2 boxes with color A

3 and 4 boxes with color B

5 boxes with color C

THEN, CHOOSE A THREE-COLOR OPTION:

Dots

- Color B small dots in 1 boxes
- Color B larger dots in 2 boxes
- Color C larger dots in 4 boxes

Dots and circles

- Color B large circles in 2 boxes
- Color B small dots in 1 and 2 boxes
- Color C circles with dots in 4 boxes

Lines in both directions

- Color B horizontal lines through 2 boxes
- Color B vertical lines through 1 and 2 boxes
- Color C horizontal and vertical lines through 4 boxes

Lines in one direction

- Color B horizontal lines through tops and bottoms of 2 boxes
- Color B horizontal lines through centers of 1 and 2 boxes
- Color C three horizontal lines through 4 boxes

FOR ALL FOUR-COLOR LAYERED METHODS, BEGIN BY FILLING IN:

Blank and 1 boxes with color A

2 and 3 boxes with color B

4 and 5 boxes with color C

THEN, CHOOSE A FOUR-COLOR OPTION:

- Medium-size dots
- Circles with small dots
- Starbursts
- Hashtags
- Lines in one direction
- Lines in both directions

AND COMPLETE YOUR CHOSEN OPTION BY DRAWING IT IN THE BOXES AS FOLLOWS:

Draw in 1 boxes with color B

Draw in 3 boxes with color C

Draw in 5 boxes with color D

■ Halftone Dots Method

Using a big brush tip marker in one color, dot the grid with dots ranging from small to large, the sizes varying depending on how hard you press. You can make very small dots in blank boxes, if you like, or leave them blank. If you have trouble with the marker ink bleeding and filling in the white space with groups of 4 boxes, try making dots in every other 4 box, like a checkerboard pattern; let those dry; then go back and dot in the remaining boxes.

You can make the halftone dots with multiple colors using shades ranging medium to dark, but don't choose anything too light.

- 1: small dot
- 2: slightly larger dot
- 3: larger dot that doesn't touch box edges
- 4: large dot that touches edges with white space at corners
- 5: very large dot, outside edges with no white space

■ Pen Drawing Methods

All of the following methods, which make darker values by drawing more pen lines, work best with a medium pen tip, around .5 mm. Your lines in the 5 boxes shouldn't leave very much white space. For these methods, each box is drawn in individually (don't make lines that travel from one box through to the next), but it's fine if the drawings go outside the box boundary lines a little.

You can take this concept and get super artistic with it by drawing little pictures, such as flowers or abstract doodles, ranging from light to dark. Use a very fine point (.2 mm) to get finer detail.

Circles

- 1: small dot
- 2: small circle
- 3: medium-size circle with dot
- 4: large circle, smaller circle, and dot
- 5: solid large dot

Starbursts

- 1: small dot
- 2: small X
- 3: larger asterisk
- 4: four lines going corner to corner, top to bottom, side to side
- 5: dense lines out from center to borders with little white space

Short lines

- 1: one line
- 2: two lines
- 3: three lines
- 4: four lines
- 5: five lines

Hashtags

1: one vertical line

2: two horizontal lines

3: two vertical and two horizontal lines

4: two vertical and four horizontal lines

5: five vertical and five horizontal lines

■ Continuous Lines Methods

These methods work by adding more lines across boxes as the numbers get higher, so that the 1 boxes have a single line and the 5 boxes have five to eight lines, depending on which option you're using. Lines are drawn through all applicable touching boxes without stopping, so you end up with long lines running across the art. On the final step, you'll draw lines through every box on the page except blanks and ✕ boxes.

Always start by scanning over the page and drawing lines through just the 5 boxes, then going back through the whole picture and drawing lines through the 4 boxes and the 5 boxes, picking up your pen whenever you hit a lower number. Then add new lines to the 3 boxes and the 4 and 5 boxes, and so on. If you miss a box on one step but spot it on the next time through, just add the missing lines, no problem.

Directions of lines can be changed, flipping horizontal and vertical, or switching directions of diagonal lines. And don't worry about lines being super straight or perfect—this art is meant to look like you created it, not a computer!

You can make a many-colored line picture by using a different color for each step. If your colors are all around the same darkness level, there's no need to range from light to dark in terms of which colors are used for which boxes. However, if some of your colors are darker than others, use the darkest colors for the first steps (the highest numbers). It's best if none of the colors used in this method are very light, so avoid yellows and pale shades.

Continuous lines #1

Best with a thick pen or fine point marker, around 1 mm or a bit finer

5 boxes: vertical left and horizontal bottom

4 boxes and all boxes with lines: vertical right

3 boxes and all boxes with lines: horizontal top

2 boxes and all boxes with lines: horizontal centered

1 boxes and all boxes with lines: vertical centered

Continuous lines #2

Best with a medium point pen, around .5 mm

5 boxes: diagonal in both directions

4 boxes and all boxes with lines: vertical on both sides

3 boxes and all boxes with lines: horizontal on top and bottom

2 boxes and all boxes with lines: vertical centered

1 boxes and all boxes with lines: horizontal centered

Continuous lines #3

Best with a medium point or thicker pen, .5–1 mm

5 boxes: horizontal and vertical along all four sides

4 boxes and all boxes with lines: diagonal in one direction

3 boxes and all boxes with lines: diagonal in the other direction

2 boxes and all boxes with lines: vertical centered

1 boxes and all boxes with lines: horizontal centered

Continuous lines #4

Best with a medium point pen, around .5 mm

5 boxes: horizontal centered and diagonal in one direction

4 boxes and all boxes with lines: vertical left and diagonal in the other direction

3 boxes and all boxes with lines: horizontal top and vertical right

2 boxes and all boxes with lines: horizontal bottom

1 boxes and all boxes with lines: vertical centered

Continuous lines #5

Best with a medium point pen, around .5 mm

5 boxes: horizontal along top edge

4 boxes and all boxes with lines: horizontal top of center

3 boxes and all boxes with lines: horizontal bottom of center

2 boxes and all boxes with lines: horizontal along bottom edge

1 boxes and all boxes with lines: horizontal centered

■ Grouped Methods

These work best with a very fine point pen (around .2 mm) and markers in six colors.

With your pen, draw larger boxes or ovals around groups of boxes of the same number (including blanks); there is no right or wrong way to do this, as long as all the numbers within a shape are the same number. You may choose to not make any grouped shapes wider than two or three boxes, or you can make them larger.

You'll have lots of single box shapes and narrow groups, one box wide. Some images may end up being mostly narrow groups without a lot of bigger shapes, but it will still look cool!

First, make the groups with either ovals or rectangles:

Rounded rectangle examples

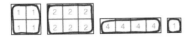

Sharp rectangle examples

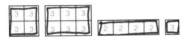

Oval examples

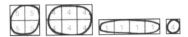

Separate numbers into ovals or rectangles like this: 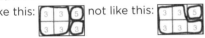 not like this:

You may then choose to make small or narrow holes in large shapes (more than 1 box across in both directions) like this:

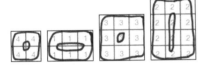

You may also make rings in very large groups (three or more boxes across in both directions) by drawing three loops inside the group, then filling them in like this:

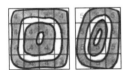

Once your groups are drawn, fill them in with six colors, using the same light-to-dark color rules as with any other method.

■ Stamping Methods

These methods are similar to the six-color large dots method (page 4), but using stamps instead of markers. For all these options except the halftone dots, follow the color instructions on page 4 using six colors.

Using a full pencil eraser:

Using a pencil eraser erased around the edges to make a smaller circle:

Using a pencil eraser with four sides cut off to make a square:

Using a set of five pencil erasers, carved into varying sizes, imitating the halftone dots method (page 5), using one ink color for all boxes:

1: smallest

2: slightly larger

3: almost touching edges

4: touching all edges

5: outside all edges

Using letter stamps, varying a bit in size as well as in ink color, for light to dark:

Blank: stamp with minimal lines, lightest color

1: slightly more lines and slightly darker

2: slightly more lines and slightly darker

3: medium amount of lines, slightly darker

4: medium amount of lines, slightly darker

5: most lines, darkest color

NOTE: Avoid letters with large empty centers, such as C, O, or D. A or B would be okay.

FINISHING YOUR WORK

When you're finished, hold the picture away from your face or step across the room to best see the image. You could also look at the page through your camera phone screen, so it shrinks down smaller, or it may help you see the picture better if you turn it sideways.

If you don't love how your finished image turned out, try adding a layer! If you colored it with markers, you could add continuous lines with a pen over the top—use an extra fine point pen if you want the color to show through more. Or if you used a pen method, fill in the boxes with colors; just filling in all the blank and number boxes with one single color in a light shade to give the object a silhouette outline will make it pop!

Another way to make your image stand out is to layer halftone dots over the six-color filled in method, making the dots with the color that was used for 5 boxes (this was the method used to make the cover image). It also looks cool to layer a continuous lines method, with a fine point pen, over halftone dots, with the dots in a medium or bright color.

After you've completed any pen method so the image has appeared on the page, you could also color in the image with multiple colors based on the object itself instead of the numbered squares. For example, color the sunflower with a brown center, yellow petals, and green leaves.

Now that you've tested out your tools and techniques on scrap paper, and chosen some methods you want to try out, it's time to start coloring, dashing, and dotting your way to this awesome art. The techniques might feel weird at first, but once you get started, it can be addictive! Let's see what you make!

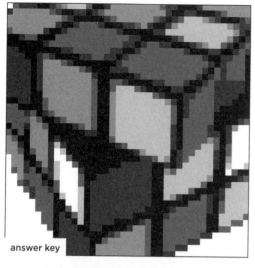

answer key

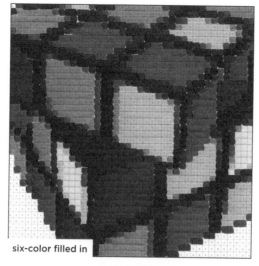

six-color filled in

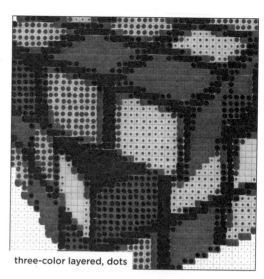

three-color layered, dots

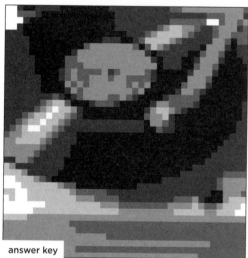

answer key

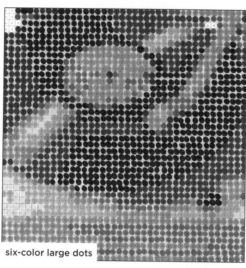

six-color large dots

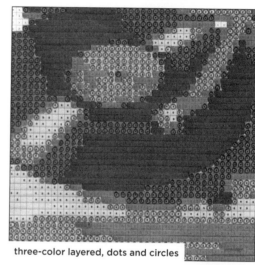

three-color layered, dots and circles

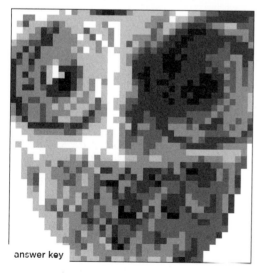

answer key

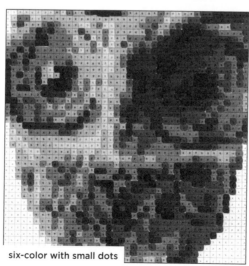

six-color with small dots

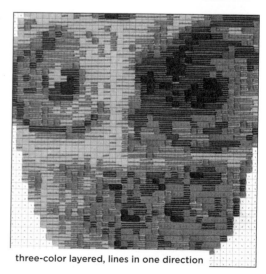

three-color layered, lines in one direction

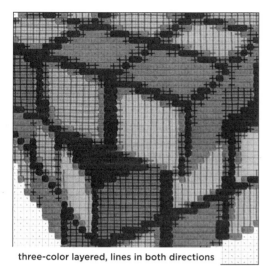

three-color layered, lines in both directions

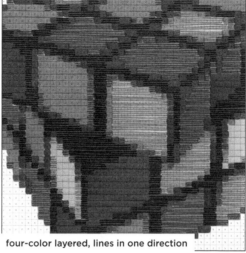

four-color layered, lines in one direction

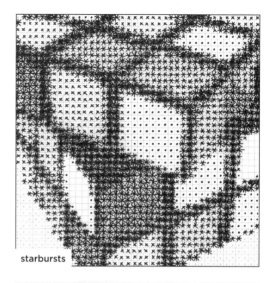

starbursts

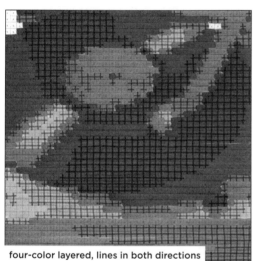

four-color layered, lines in both directions

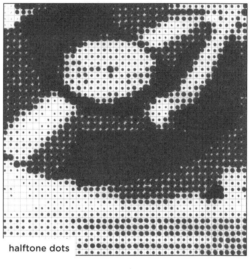

halftone dots

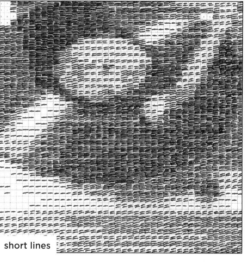

short lines

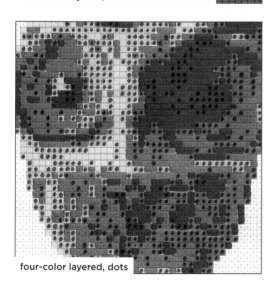

four-color layered, dots

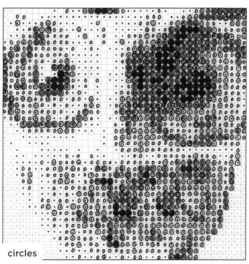

circles

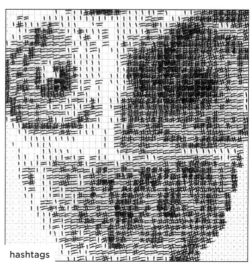

hashtags

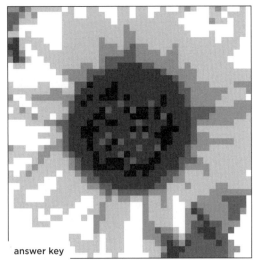

answer key

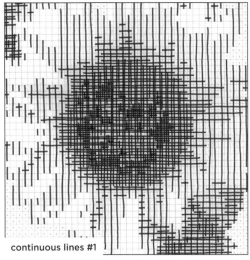

continuous lines #1

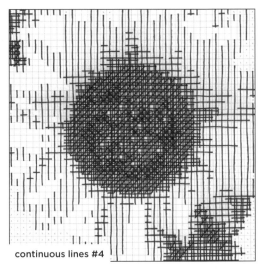

continuous lines #4

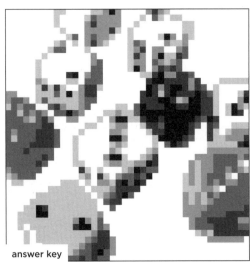

answer key

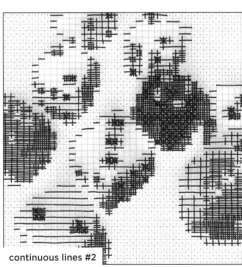

continuous lines #2

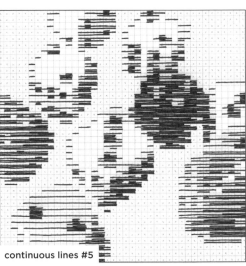

continuous lines #5

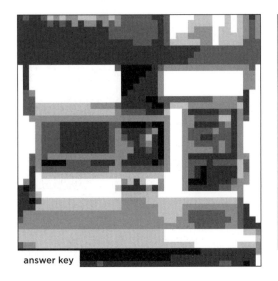

answer key

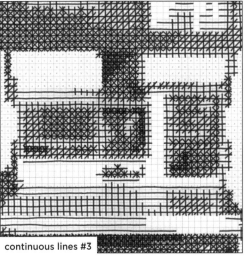

continuous lines #3

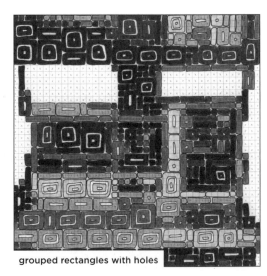

grouped rectangles with holes

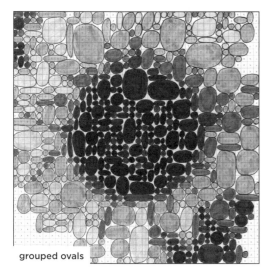

grouped ovals

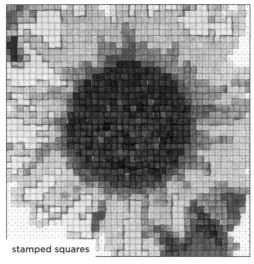

stamped squares

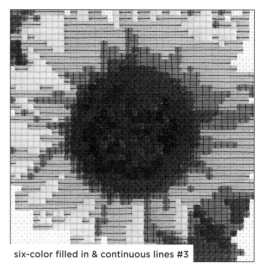

six-color filled in & continuous lines #3

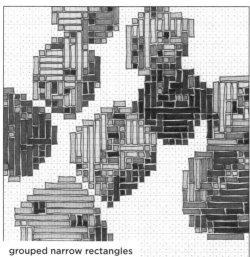

grouped narrow rectangles

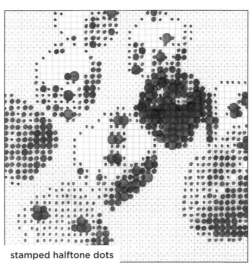

stamped halftone dots

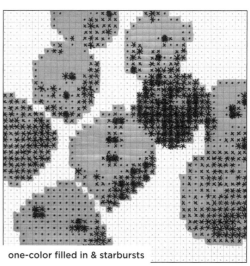

one-color filled in & starbursts

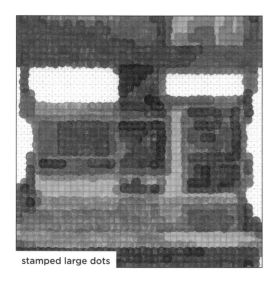

stamped large dots

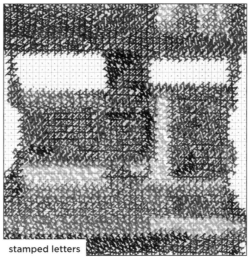

stamped letters

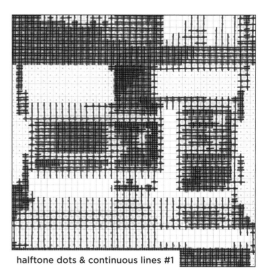

halftone dots & continuous lines #1

Practice Grids

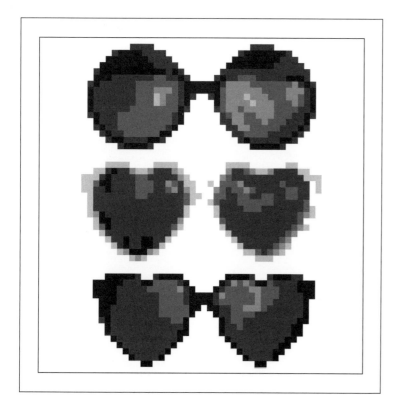

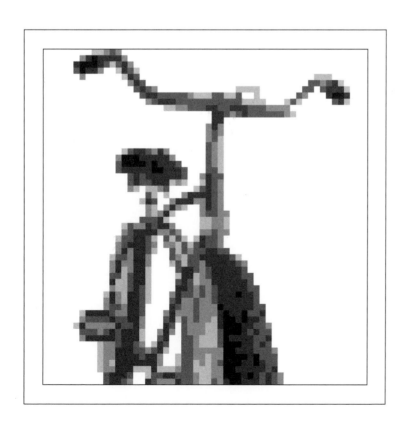

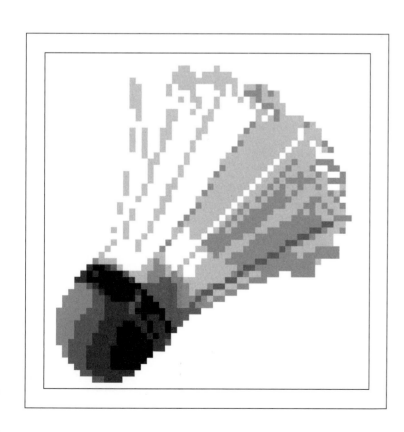

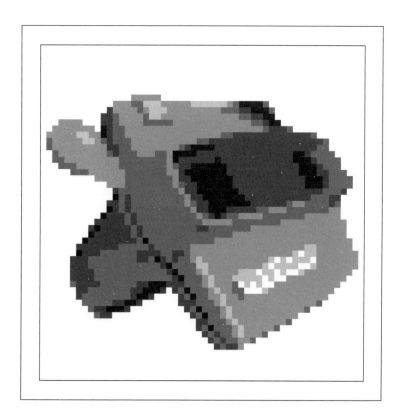

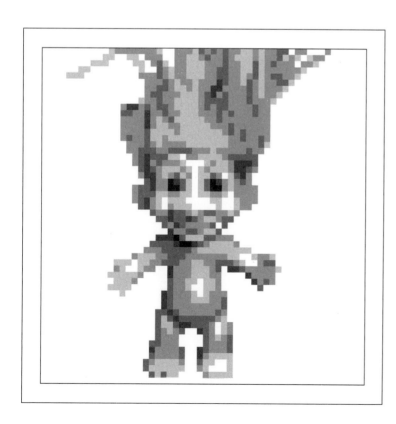

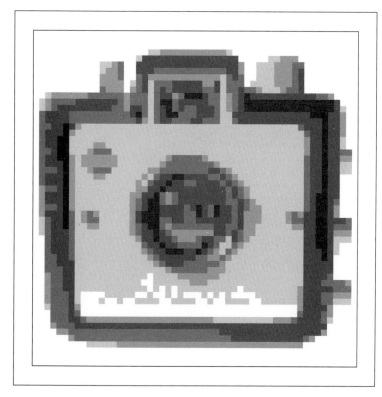

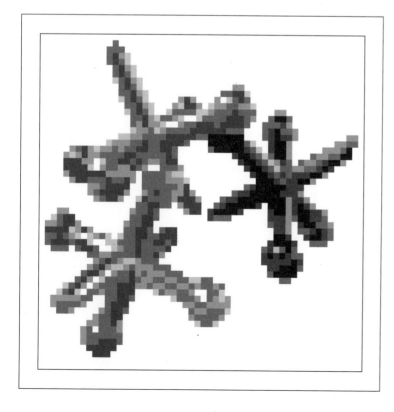

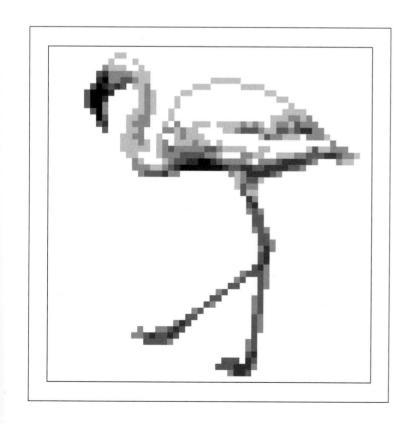

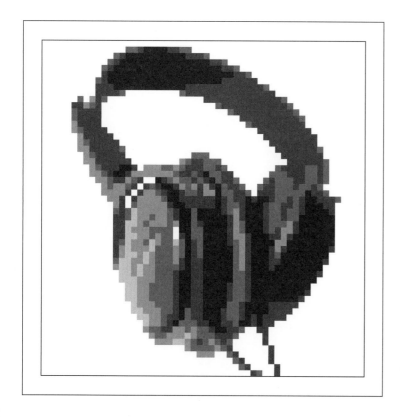

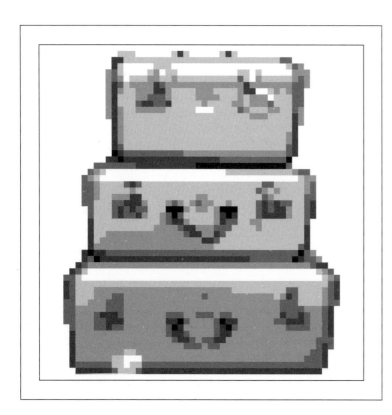

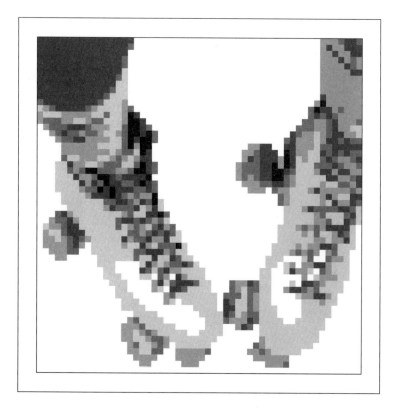

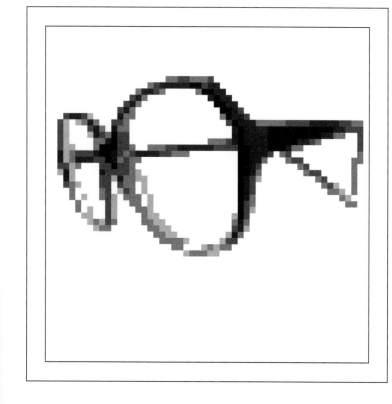

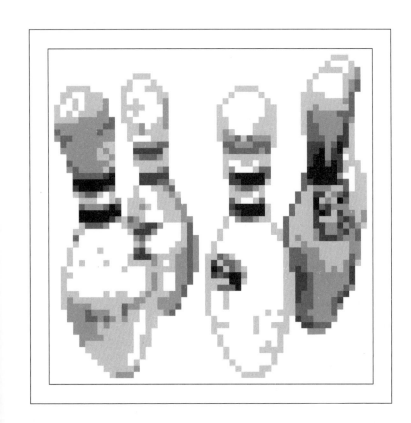

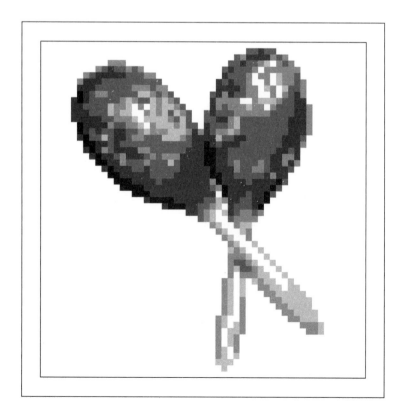

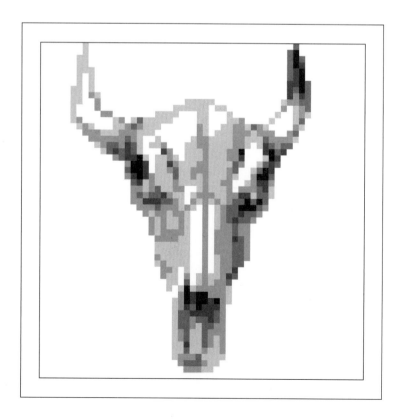

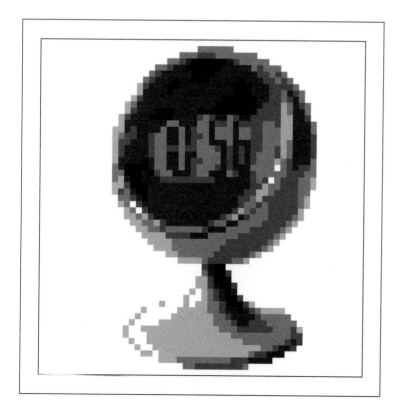

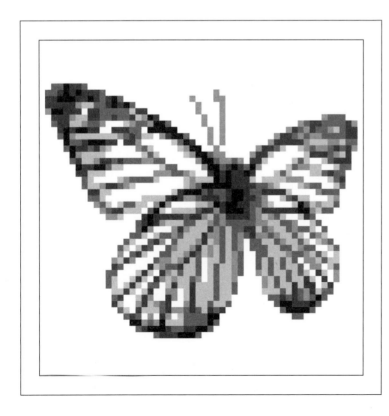

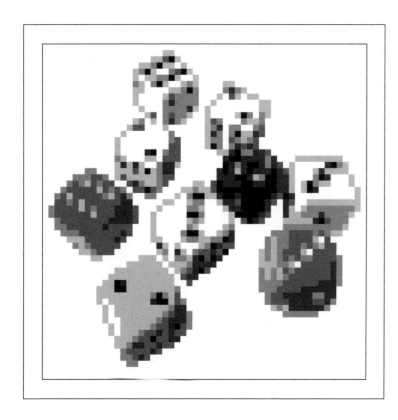

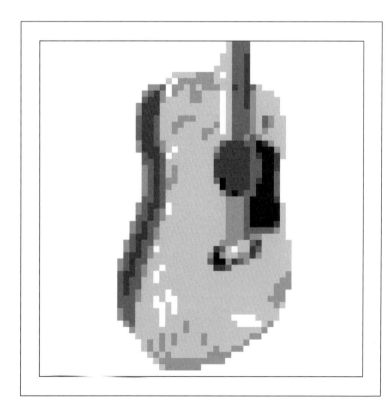

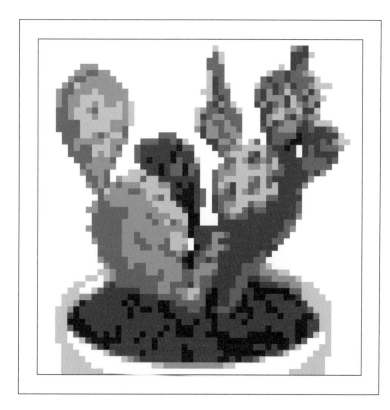

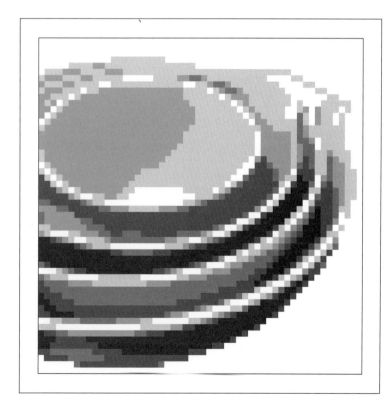

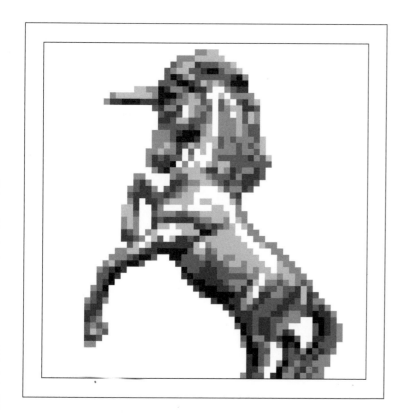

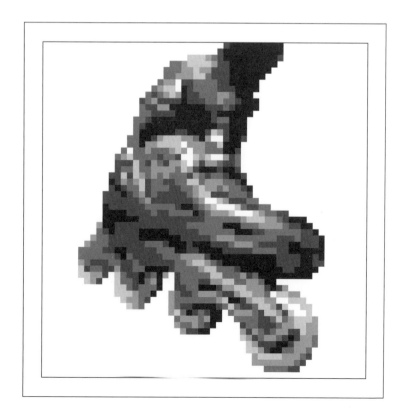

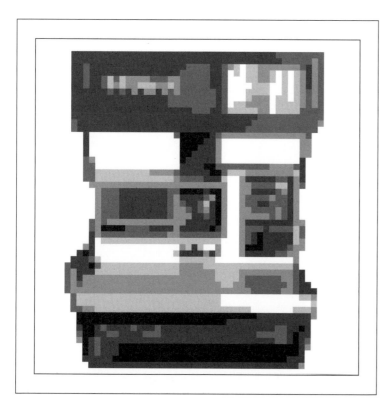

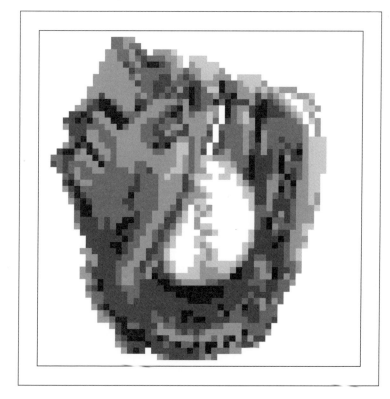

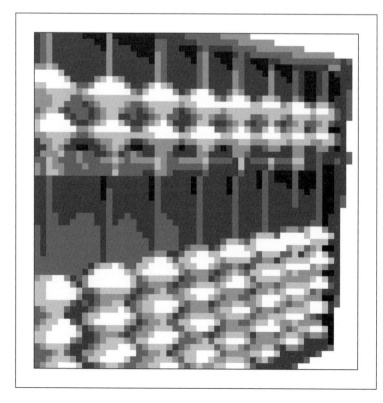

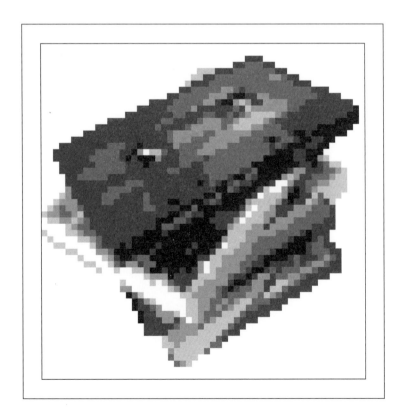

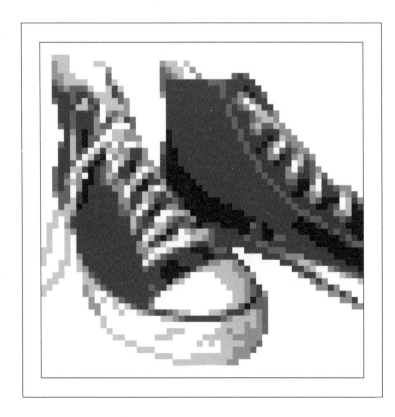

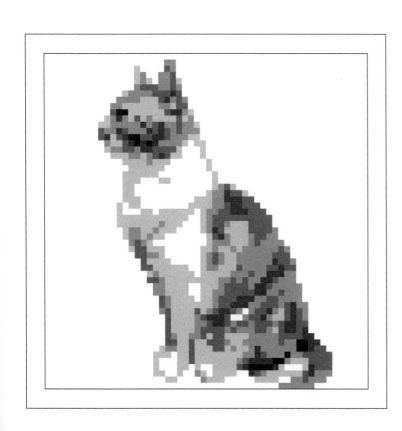

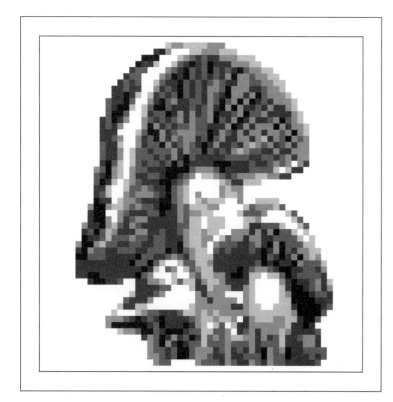

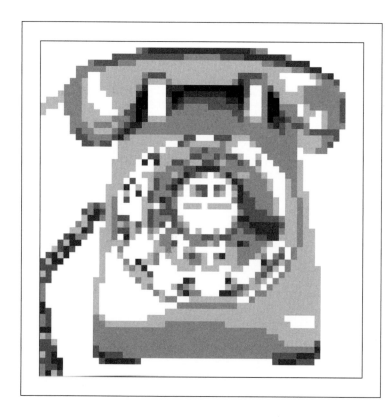

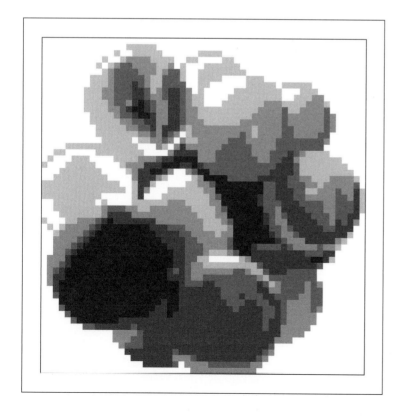

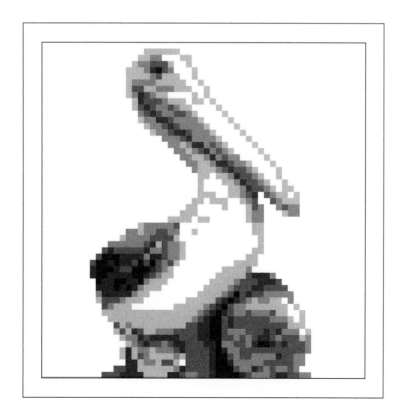

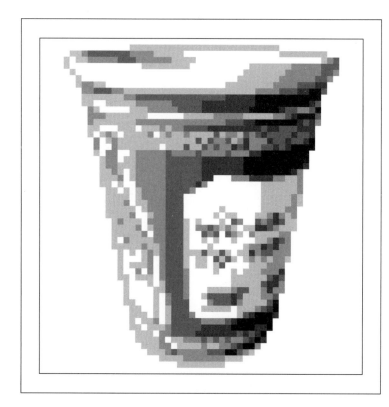

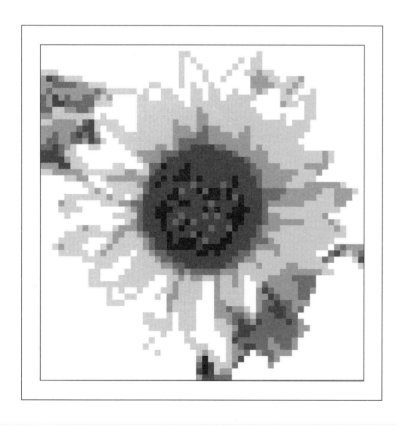

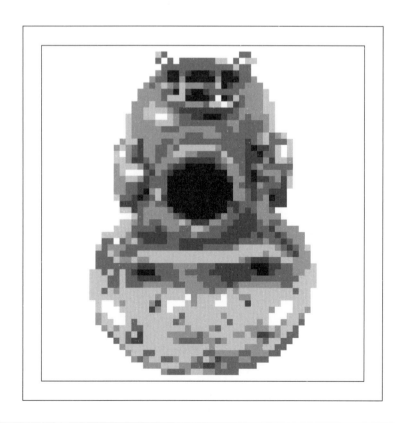

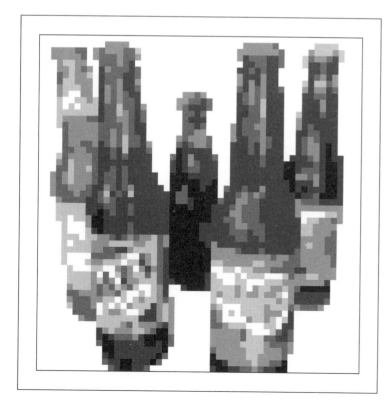

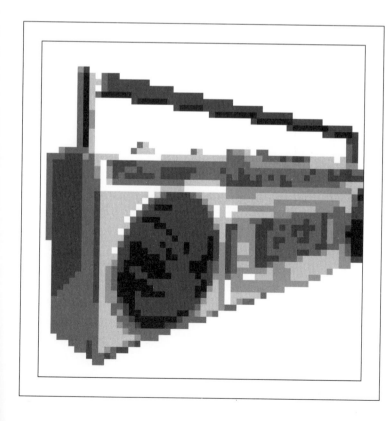

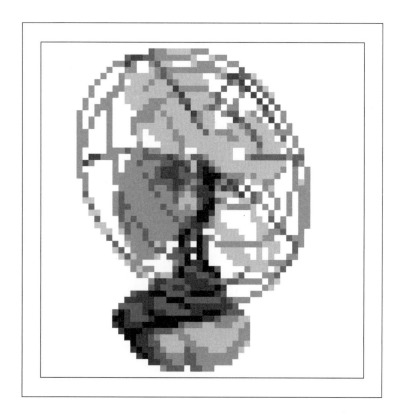

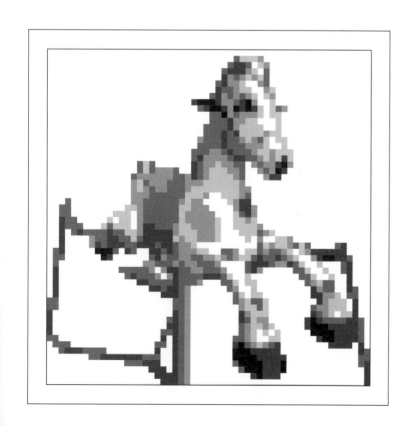

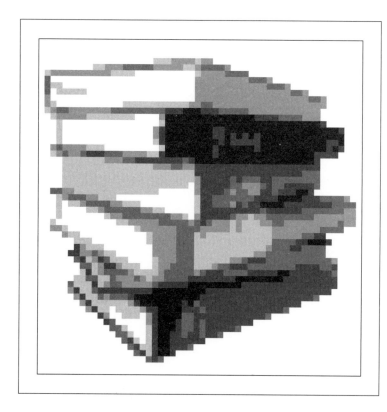

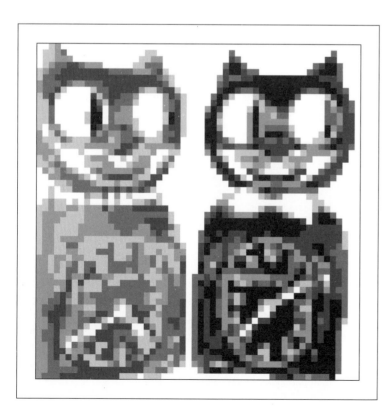

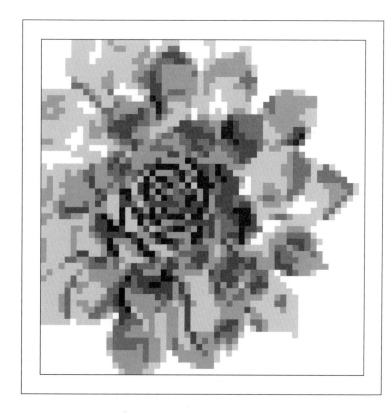

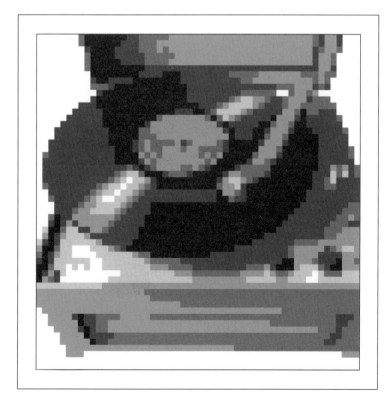

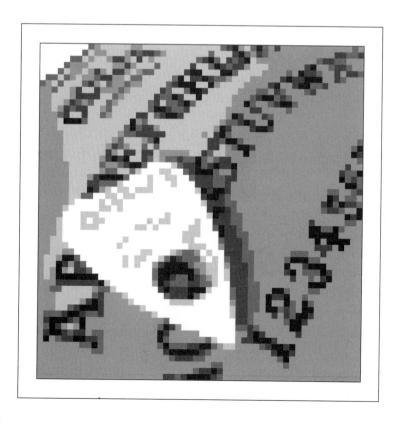

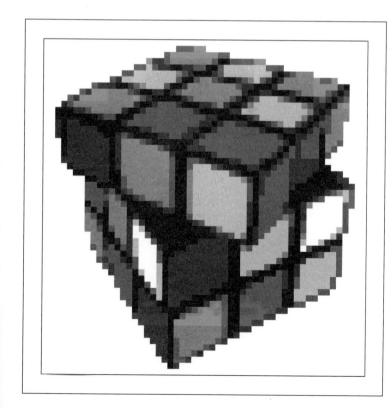

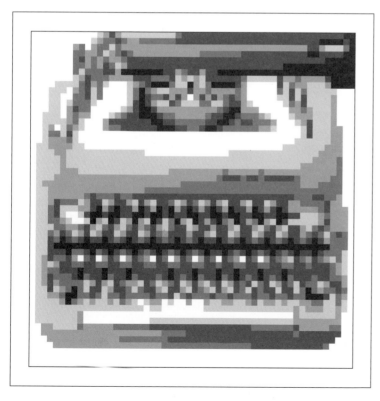

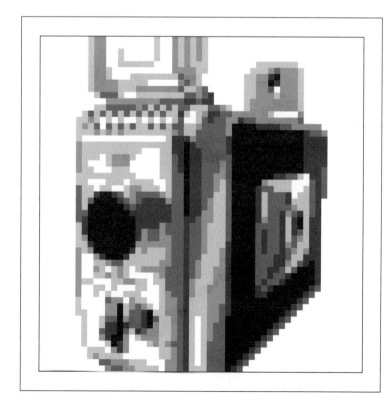

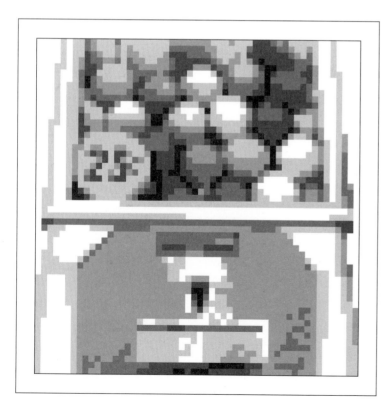

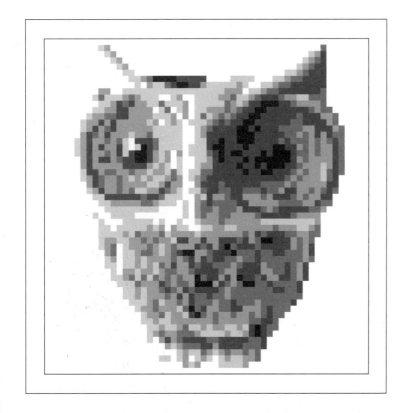